The Bloomington Academy

The first British curriculum institution in the Emirate of Ajman, which is also easily accessible from Sharjah and Umm Al Quwain. The school, with a rapidly increasing student strength representing 70+ different nationalities, has grown over the years into an edifice of modern education with all the latest technological teaching and learning support systems. The students are at the heart of all processes in the school, and all school operations are aimed at helping them grow into confident individuals whose innate talents and abilities are identified, strengthened, and nurtured during their precious learning years. The school is affiliated to the CAIE (Cambridge Assessment International Education – of the University of Cambridge, UK), and therefore follows the prestigious Cambridge Curriculum.

One of the strongest features of the institution that has helped it gain acceptance and acclaim in society, is the international standards of education that the school offers at an extremely competitive price. Facilities and resources available are worthy of an international institution and support a holistic and comprehensive education that emphasizes upon, not only the acquisition of knowledge but also skill development and problem solving, such that students are able to utilize their learning in the real world through reflection and understanding.

English Language
Bloomerang
A Kaleidoscope of Tales and Verses
(Stories & Poems)
by
Bloom Authors

Published in November 2023
by Decan Imprint Publishing Co.
Reg. Off: Sharjah Publishing City
Free Zone Sharjah, UAE.
Phone: 00971-551830334
Email : decanimprint@gmail.com

Cover Design : Aromal O P

Printed at
Manipal Technologies Ltd.

10/23-24/Sl.No.10/150/NS 18.6
ISBN 978-93-5973-866-6

BLOOMERANG
A Kaleidoscope of Tales and Verses

Bloom Authors

DECANIMPRINT

CHAIRMAN'S MESSAGE

Mr. Lanson Lazar

Language and Literature have always been the foundation and pillars of cultural understanding, artistic expression, and intellectual growth. This compilation embodies the vibrant tapestry of our students' literary work.

I extend my sincere appreciation and gratitude to the editors and reviewers who worked diligently in bringing this work to fruition. Their meticulous attention to detail and commitment to academic excellence have assured the quality and significance of this publication. May this compiled version of articles ignite your passion for language and literature, provoke new heights and inspire lifelong love for the written word.

Writers, editors, proofreaders, designers, and many others have dedicated their time and expertise to ensure quality and integrity of the content.

I would like to express my deepest gratitude to our student writers whose passion and dedication have made this publication a reality. Your contributions, dear students, have enriched the literary landscape. Creativity has no limits, hence the transformation of this literary landscape will continue.

Together let us continue to embrace our students' passion for writing to build a brighter future for them, as well as for society.

CEO's MESSAGE
Ms. Sandra Blaskovic

Language, the cornerstone of human communication, be it spoken or written, has the power to shape societies, bridge cultural gaps and unlock profound potential.

It is with great pleasure that we present this significant literary work of our students. From the preliminary conception of the idea to the final publication, the journey of this book has been a collaborative effort involving several passionate individuals.

I would like to express my deepest gratitude to our student writers, whose love for writing has made this anthology a reality. Their contributions have enriched the literary panorama and expanded imaginary horizons, at the same time our writers will enjoy increased visibility and valuable experience. This compilation not only celebrates creativity and expression but is also aimed at making it a reader's delight.

Thank you for joining us on this intellectual literary journey, a testimony to the enduring value of literature. Together let us celebrate the beauty, complexity and love of language and embrace its transformative power in shaping the world.

PRINCIPAL'S MESSAGE
Ms. Hussaina Begum Noor Sherieff

MULTIVERSA

"Bloomerang: A Kaleidoscope of Tales and Verses" is a wonderful and imaginative title for an anthology that showcases the creative writing talents of students at The Bloomington Academy Private School in Ajman, UAE.

This title not only captures the essence of the diverse cultural backgrounds of the students but also the vibrant and varied nature of their literary works. It suggests a rich blend of stories, poems, and experiences that come together to create a captivating and dynamic collection.

CONTENTS

YELLOW SUNSHINE
Simal M. Kabir (Gr.5A2)

As yellow as the sunshine
You welcomed us one by one,
You were always ready and eager
To have a ne day of fun.
Purple is for the patience
You have shown throughout the year,
Helping us through our problems
And making them all so clear
The Colour red represents our class
And all the friends we've made
And Green is for the colour go
As we move up to the next grade.
Blue is how we feel
Knowing the year must end
We wish you a happy summer
And well wishes we do send.

THE SCHOOL TRIP TO FUN LAND
Mohammad Huzaifa (Gr. 6B1)

I was sleeping comfortably with my warm blanket covering me and making me feel warm.

I was dreaming about our trip to fun land when all of a sudden, I heard my mom's voice "Huzaifa Dear, wake up its 6.00am, and you will be late for school." I jumped out of my bed with excitement, as it was a trip day. After brushing my teeth, I got ready for school with my lunch bag. I dressed up and brushed my hair. I packed my bag with my favorite snacks, Chocolate, and drinks.

I said goodbye to my mom and dad before going to the bus. We reached school, and then our teacher, after giving us instructions, asked us to be seated on another bus. We all were happy, and our way, many beautiful places passed by before we reached our location, we kept on chatting and enjoying in the bus. At last, we were at the door of fun land. A big green centipede Ferris wheel welcomed us when we went inside the fun land Me, and my friends were looking around to find the roller coaster that is called the rook star coaster. We found the Rook Star Coaster we sat in.

MY FAVOURITE FOOD
Liba Hasnain (Gr. 6A2)

My fovourite food is Chicken Biriyani. It is served with gravy and raita. It is a flavorful dish that has a rich taste. It is famous Pakistan Subcontinent dish that is popular around the world. Basmati rice is combined with various spices and cooked uniquely to make Biriyani. This meal has a deep taste and is filled with flavor. Biriyani, a harmonious blend of spices, meat, rice, and an indescribable sense of satisfaction, is my favourite food. The origins of this delectable dish can be traced back to Pakistani subcontinent, where it was first concocted by the Mughais.

The top layer is often garnished with fried onions, boiled eggs, or fresh herds like coriander and mint. The spices used, such as turmeric, cumin, and garam masala, give the dish its distinctive aroma and taste. Some people also add Yogurt or Tomatoes to make it savorier. Hyderbadi biriyani in Indian it consists of goat meat that's marinated and further cooked with rice, along with coconut and saffron seasoning. Sindhi Biriyani is a north Pakistan recipe made using mutton, basmati rice, Yoghurt, onions, green chilies, potatoes, and tomatoes. This main dish is a mélange of spices like turmeric powder and paprika. Cinnamon, cardamoms, and dried plums. It is a great dish for buffets, partles or dlnners.

BEAUTIFUL DAY
Dreanna Kendra Koruwage (Gr. 5A2)

What a beautiful day
To go outside.
Let's laugh and
Leap in the sun
The grass is green.
The sky is blue,
Let's go and have some fun!

FRIENDS
Mary Martha (Gr. 6A)

Life is a broken road.
Full of breakers and bends
When the Journey feels
Too much
The Week may be full of
Mondays but there'll
Always be weekends
When people let you down
Take comfort in a friend!

MY FRIEND
Noor Rafiq (Gr. 6A2)

One of them is Hafsa. Her favourite colour is red and black. Her Zodiac sign is Cancer. She loves all the food items in the world. She does not know yet what she wants to become in her future. Her age is 12 years. She is born on July 22 in the year 2011. She has brown pretty hair; her eyes are also brown like a pet cat.

My second friend is Maryam. Her favourite colour is sky blue, I too love sky blue, and I love her. Her Zodiac sign is Leo. Her favourite food is Roman. She wants to become a Surgeon in her future. She promised me that she will work for the poor needy people. Her age is 10, She was born on August 12 in the year 2013. Her hair is dark brown and brown eyes look just like a squirrel's. She is a very kind person.

Third is Afra. Her favourite colour is red and black. Her Zodiac sign is Libra. She loves all the food in the world. She does not know yet what she wants to become in her future. Her age is 9. She is born on October 4 in the year 2013. She has brown hair like the tale of fillies, her eyes are brown too.

WHAT I WANT TO BE
Musfira Fatima (Gr. 6B2)

I really want to be a fashion designer. Why?

Because I really love to make clothes combine to a new style and show it to everyone and also, I want to show everyone that fashion is good and awesome making our own combine and making that style being a model designer is very easy. You just need to use your imagination in your mind and make it a fashion.

Show it to everyone and impress them that clothes can be another style, and everyone can do it as well! We just all need to use our mind not to steal another style try to make your own style and everyone might love your design and around the world will try to make their own style too. So don't think that fashion designers are hard just use your mind.

A FISH POEM
Izzah Khan (Gr. 5A2)

How I wish
I were a Fish.
My day would begin,
Flapping my fins.
I'd make a commotion,
Out in the ocean.
It would be cool,
To swim in a school.
In the sea,
I'd move so free,
With just one thought
Don't get caught.

PRINCE GIRL
Pima Kik (Gr. 5A2)

There was a girl, who was hungry,
So, she went to a cottage.
She saw a big bear.
The bear roared.
She got scared, but then the bear said,
"I am not going to hurt you!"
Then it said, "Make me a potion,
To turn me human again."
She said, "I will make the potion,
But don't hurt me."
He said, "Make it and I will marry you."
She made the potion and
It suddenly turned into a Prince.

AUTOBIOGRAPHY OF MYSELF
Rital Mansour (Gr. 5A2)

Hi, my name is Rital Mansour, and I am 11 years old. I am currently writing this on 14th of September 2023. I was born on the 10th of June 2012 and my favourite colours are light pink, sky blue and white. I have a family of four members. My Dad, my Mom, my brother and me. I also have a lot of cousins and aunts and uncles as well as grandparents. I love my family so much because they are supportive, loving, and caring. In the day that I am free in I usually do something fun, like playing, drawing, and doing sports and more things. Every Friday me, my parents, and my brother we go to a garden between Sharjah and Ajman, the garden is so big and beautiful and has a scent of flowers, and in other days of the week we do something else like studying, playing, working and even more fun and important things, sometimes we go get Ice cream my favorite ice-cream flavor is vanilla and strawberry. That's how I spend the weekend when I have school, but when I don't have school like in the summerholidays, I do something more fun like travelling, going to hotels and things that are fun. That's all. I hope you enjoyed reading it.

MY TRIP TO LEGO LAND
Yumna Khan (Gr. 5A2)

It was a very hot day when there was a school trip to Lego Land. We sat in the classroom for a while then went outside and made a line then got inside the bus. On the way it was so noisy in the bus, all the kids were shouting and screaming like crazy. When we reached our location, everyone kept silent and rushed to get down, I was so excited. We went inside this building where there were lots of mini things and blocks, there were lots of rides there like rollercoaster water rides etc. My favourite ride was the big rollercoaster, it went so fast at the end we ate burgers and went back to school.

THE WORLD'S BEST AUNT
Anabia Aziz (Gr. 2A)

You are my world, my sunshine.
You dressed me like a princess.
You celebrated my birthday with love, my world,
my aunt dearest to me,
She is very loyal and kind to me.
You are special in my life.
I can feel her love in my dreams.
You are always in my heart!
Her prayers and wishes are with me
forever the world's best aunt is adorable,
You are the beautiful gift of God,
I want to say special thanks
that I love you a lot Ammi!

LOOKOUT FOR YOURSELF STORY
Sawiya Nabeel Malik (Gr. 9A)

Have you ever thrown a stone into the water just to see it bouncing twice? Asli has felt getting herself into the deep water and then bouncing back. One year ago, in a small town of England called 'Whitby' (Whitby is a seaside town in Yorkshire, northern England, split by the river Esk) on the East Cliff, overlooking the North Sea, the ruined Gothic Whitby Abbey was Bram Stoker's inspiration for "Dracula". Nearby is the Church of St. Mary's, to be reached by 199 steps. The Captain Cook Memorial Museum, in the house where Cook once lived, displays paintings and maps. West of the town is the West Cliff Beach line.

Once there lived a girl named Asli. She was from a middle-class family. With lofty ambitions and hard work, she wanted to be the Number 1 Heart Surgeon of England. She was the topper of her class and an obedient student, the 'apple of the eye' of her teachers. Her father, Baran, was proud of her. Since childhood she used to live with her father. Her mother died due to a heart disease which had treatment, but since it was expensive and due to the late arrangement of money, her mother died on the ventilator.

A girl like Asli was super talented, with 142 IQ level and a beautiful, charming smile. Since she was the only daughter, somehow her father was at ease to pay bills and due to her achievements, her school supplied her free of cost education from grade 8 till her high school. Moreover, her teachers and the Principal Miss Elif believed that she would get 100% scholarship.

Other than studies, Asli was the right hand of her father. If her father was doing his job during the daytime, Asli used to do job at night to balance the work and earn more to pay the bills. Asli was not a thankless girl but living in an environment where everyone is different makes one feel awkward that one is not suitable to live on this side of life. Besides Asli knew the insecurities of the people. They give up and let the gene die! She knew that she had to chin up and she wasn't the type to cry. She should awaken the hungry beast sleeping within and know that if today they are making fun of her, tomorrow they will take her as a role model.

While everything was going well, unexpectedly one day, while taking her English lecture she heard her Principal telling her favorite teacher Miss Starlight not to tell everything to Asli. At this time security guard of the school came to class with a spooky face and asked, "Who is Asli?" Asli replied, "It's me. Why? What happened?" The security guard told her the news which the Principal had told him not to tell! He said that her father had an accident near the school and that he is no more! Listening to that, Asli went pale. Of Course, her father was her first and last support person on whom she was dependent. A person who loved her and never let her experience how one feels without a mother.

Her father was her only way to survive in this cruel world where no one respects humanity but love to work practical and stay neutral. This was the worst news to hear in her all life. Asli became blank and she ran to the washroom. She stared at the mirror in front of her and she suddenly felt a pain in her heart. A sudden hot flush and she was not able to breathe. She saw her eyes turning red as if her soul was getting buried alive, her white face turned pale yellow, and she couldn't stand properly.

This was the time for her to be brave and have some patience. But when she saw the dead body of her father, covered in a white shawl, she unconsciously sat on the ground, crawling, and saying, "I must be dreaming. It isn't true." Her favourite teacher Miss Starlight gave her the support she required to stand up and be confident because they knew that if she would not be brave now, she would get sick and something terrible would happen because of her soft heart. Asli chooses to live and let go of all the negative thoughts. The time went by in a jiffy, as time and tide wait for no one.

Days passed and one year later Asli Baran received the award for achieving the highest marks in the 'International Benchmark Test! A girl with a confident face and tear-filled eyes went up on stage to receive her award. She was not nervous as she had received many awards before. This year she had 4 Trophies and 12 Gold Medals. Asli, who had no survival thoughts, instead wanted to give up in life. The only thing which kept her thriving was the promise she had given her father, that she would become the Number 1 Heart Surgeon of England. She achieved all A*s in AS and A Level. Asli went to Oxford University for higher education on a scholarship. A girl with 142 IQ level was a tough competitor of everyone since her school and then high school and now university.

Whatever Asli did during these years only she knew the sacrifice, the pain, the power she needed to prove herself and somehow, she was still doing the job which her father used to do. Whenever she gets the time, she goes to her job to get wages to pay the bills. Now Oxford University was providing them internship with payment.

After completing her medical studies, she opened her own hospital which was free of cost for poor people and cheap treatment for the ones who were accessible to pay later. She was the best heart surgeon not only in England besides worldwide. Of Course, after the difficult time comes the good times. Her whole journey was about a lesson that tough times come, and one should stand strong as a mountain. This is a lesson to all students worldwide that:

FOREVER RUNNING AND WORKING TO BE NUMBER 1. DON'T EVER GIVE UP AND I PROMISE YOU WILL BE ON THE TOP. WHATEVER

YOU SEEK, JUST KEEP ON TRYING. NOBODY CAN STOP YOU. GET IT OUT OF YOUR BRAIN JUST BECAUSE YOU FAIL DOESN'T MEAN YOU CAN'T STAND UP AGAIN. KEEP MOVING ON WITH PERSEVERANCE. LIFE IS NOT A BED OF ROSES, THERE ARE THORNS TOO!

THE ONLY THING WHICH SHE WAS PROUD OF WAS THAT, THE MANY TIMES, she stood back, it did not mean that it was the end of the world as a great Persian Poet Rumi says, "You are the entire ocean in a drop". This is what made Asli strong. For the past years, she was really motivated. She was a perfect example for the quote that: if you throw me to the pack of wolves, I will come back leading the pack! Asli tells us that life moves on and time never waits for anyone. She learnt that one must be like the person who leads the pack and walk alone with faith. "Challenging work is easy but having faith is hard".

FAITH
Eman Fatima Nouman (Gr. 9A)

Two friends, who had just landed in Saudi Arabia, one of the holiest and largest countries in the Arab and Muslim world.

Sam and Alex went to check in their hotel rooms, Sam was studying medicine and Alex was in the field of dentistry. Both were studying in the same college which led them to form their bond of friendship, and now, they are going to pursue their studies in the same university.

They got their keycards and checked in their hotel room. It wasn't very big since it was a temporary space provided by the university. Sam thought that there was no point in unpacking, so he went straight to bed meanwhile Alex had already started to unpack.

"We still have a week before university starts, let me sleep" Sam said to Alex who had been trying to wake him up for the last 30 minutes.

"It's already 1pm!" Alex said with a hint of annoyance in his voice.

"Fine fine." Sam finally gave in.

They both had planned to explore this "new world" before burying themselves in their studies.

They left their rooms at 1:56pm, grabbed something to eat on their way out, asked for directions which was near impossible because of the language barrier and finally, they had arrived.

"Whoa! This temple is enormous!" Samyelled, admiring the scenery set before his eyes.

"It's a mosque not a temple." Alex whispered in embarrassment.

They were visiting King Khalid Great Mosque in Riyadh because of its 4.8-star rating and also because it wasn't too far.

They took off their shoes, stepped in and the exploration began.

It was their first time seeing a mosque from both inside and outside.

"Whoa the roof is so high, or is it even a roof?" Sam blabbered on and on in excitement. Alex nodded in agreement.

A tourist guide approached them. He greeted the two boys and offered to give them a tour. Sam agreed without wasting a single second.

They learned a lot about Islam, the pillars, how to perform wudu, offer salah and so on.

It was time for Asr. The boy's ears picked up a beautiful sound. "What is that sound?" Alex asked in admiration. That was the first question from Alex.

"It's the sound of the Adhan." The tourist replied. "The Imam says the Adhan, informing us when it's time to pray."

"You get to hear this beautiful n' elegant voice 5 times a day?" Sam asked.

The tourist nodded in reply.

Both of their souls were drawn towards the voice of the Imam.

The Adhan came to an end and the boys were lost for words; they had never heard anything like it before.

The tour came to an end. "Thank you for the wonderful tour and the valuable information." Alex said, shaking his hand and Sam followed.

They decided to explore some more before getting something to eat. As they walked out of the mosque, their eyes followed a brown-haired kid with hazel eyes sitting across the road. The boy's clothes were torn and dirty, his shoes were small on his feet, he looked weak and small.

They crossed the road and went up to the boy.

The boy greeted them with a smile on his face and they greeted him back. The boy seemed to speak and understand English.

"Where are your parents? Do you have anything to eat or drink?" Sam asked with worry.

The boy smiled and replied, "If my lord wishes, he'll provide me with food and drink."

The boys glanced at each other. "When was the last time you ate?" Alex asked.

"Today in the morning."

"So, you haven't eaten almost all day?" Sam asked.

"I'm fasting." The boy replied, "It's better than starving, my lord provides me food when I intend to fast and when it's time for breaking it."

"Who is your lord?" Sam asked with confusion on why this boy trusted his lord so much.

"My lord, my guardian, my protector and my savior is, the one and only Allah, he never lets me starve, gives me the energy to move, the ability to read, write and he protects me in every step I take."

Sam and Alex started to tear up at this little boy who could be around 6-8, having this much faith in his God. They wanted to know him more, provide him shelter and food but they knew that Allah, who the guide referred to as the most merciful, will provide him with something even greater. They gave him money to buy himself something because that was the leastthey could do.

They arrived in their rooms, the words of the boy repeating in their head repeatedly like a recording. He protects me in every step I take.

"Islam is so beautiful." Sam muttered.

"Indeed." Alex replied.

Both were at a loss for words.

The two souls were touched by the young boy's words and his faith. The thought of converting crossed their minds but they thought they weren't capable enough. They decided to go back to the mosque, get proper guidance and when the time felt right, they would convert.

MARY'S TIME TRAVEL!!
Eishal Atif (Gr. 9A)

Mary Redwood: A simple girl trying her level best to save her friends.
Kate Davidson: A very sweet classmate of Mary and her friends.
Henry Williams: An athletic boy who the whole school likes, good at basketball. Friend of Mary.
Lucas Hawkins: He is the right hand of Henry.
Violet Greste: A very shy girl with social anxiety.

CHAPTER 1
MARY'S DIARY

7th September 2023

It's been two years... Since I visited my home country, I finally came back here. After coming back here, all I wanted was to meet my friends again. I tried contacting them, but I failed.

8th September 2023

I still remember the days I spent with them. We were a group of four and the whole university knew how strong our friendship was. We used to bunk classes, eat lunch while the teacher was teaching and most of the time, we were in the detention room. But after graduation our connection broke and we stopped talking to each other. I went to Canada for a job. I started missing them a lot and I wanted to meet them desperately, so I came back here to Paris, but the saddest thing was I couldn't meet them.

CHAPTER 2
MEETING OLD CLASSMATE

The alarm bell rings .... Mary wakes up and makes breakfast for herself. After completing her breakfast, she took a shower to relax herself. Just when she came out of the shower the doorbell rang. "Huh!? Who could it be at the door?". She opens the door and sees a very familiar face; IT WAS HER CLASSMATE, Kate, the very sweet girl. "Kate? How come you are here?" She was surprised to see her at her door. "I got to know that you came back to Paris, so I came to meet you," Kate said smiling. Mary called her inside and offered her coffee. They started talking about the old days of university and Mary told her how she misses them a lot. "I miss my friends a lot. do you know how hard I tried contacting them, but I failed". "Mary, did you not know?". Mary was confused and asked "What do you mean? What did I not know? Please tell me?" "Mary.... Lucas has been murdered." "What!? Who did it?" Mary was shocked. "It was Henry; he is in jail now". "What about Violet, where is she?" "Before Lucas was murdered, she committed suicide". Mary was traumatized and she was unable to utter a word! Kate received a call and she had to leave. She said goodbye to Mary and left. After Kate left, Mary was in grief, and she started crying. She thought if she had been there, she would have fixed everything, but still some questions were in her mind that bothered her a lot.

Why did Violet commit suicide?

Who murdered Lucas?

Why did Henry murder Lucas?

CHAPTER 3

THE MURDER

Mary decided to visit her friend Henry in jail, because right now he was the only one who could answer her questions. She went to the jail to visit Henry. When he saw her, he did not even say 'Hi' or ask anything to her. It looked like he was very upset with her. "Henry… why did you murder Lucas; I don't believe that you murdered him. Is that true you did it?" Henry was quiet for some time but then he spoke, "No I didn't do it, and nobody believes that." "Henry, I believe you. I'll get you out of here. Don't worry." Henry stared into her eyes and said, "I don't need your help. Get away! You were not there when we needed you." Feeling guilty she came away from the jail. While walking down the aisle, her head started spinning and she fell. When she opened her eyes while she was in the hospital. She heard the doctor saying, "Oh! Young lady, you're finally awake. You should take care of yourself, drink more water and hydrate yourself! So that this won't happen again," said the doctor. Mary nodded and smiled at the doctor. She took a taxi and went home. The taxi stopped at her place, and she started walking towards her building but then she realized that her building was nowhere to be seen. She panicked and looked here and there to make sure that she was in the right place. "I'm pretty sure that I'm at the right place, but WHERE IS MY APARTMENT!?". She took her phone to book a taxi but then she noticed something; "Why is my mobile showing the year 2022? Maybe there's a technical error with my phone." There was a newspaper lying on the ground. She picked it up only to notice that the newspaper was published on 11th April 2022. "WHAT? How is this possible?" She was very confused because the last time she remembered; it was the year 2023. She asked herself, "Am I dreaming?"

CHAPTER 4
REALIZING SHE IS NOW IN THE PAST

"It can't be true; this is not true."
Violet committed suicide on 11th April.
Does this mean I can save her?
Can I change the past now?

CHAPTER 5
FIRE IN THE APARTMENT

"As I remember Violet will be committing suicide by setting fire to her room. I should find her before night falls. I remember the area she lived in, but I don't really remember what her hotel apartment looked like." She went to the area as soon as possible. There were two buildings that she thought her friend would have been in. She went to the first building. It was going to be sunset soon. She went to the hotel and asked the receptionist, "Does a girl named Violet live here? "Receptionist: "Sorry but I can't give information about the people living here." Mary said, "You have to, it's an emergency or someone would set fire to your hotel." Receptionist: "What?" Mary: "Yes, hurry up!!". The receptionist unwillingly took Mary to Violet's room. They rang the bell and a girl came and opened the door. When Mary saw her, she said, "This is not her!" At that very moment she could hear police sirens and fire brigade reaching there. Mary looked out of the window and saw that there was a room on fire. She realized that she was a little too late to save Violet and everything started to blur in front of her! She was again at the same hospital. When she felt well, she left the hospital and went straight to Violet's hotel apartment. She went there at around 6 pm and hurried to the front office and once again asked for Violet's room number. The receptionist again refused to tell her but somehow, she convinced her, and now there were only ten minutes left. She ran to her room and rang the bell furiously. Violet opened the door and as soon as possible Mary dragged her out of the apartment. Violet: "Mary? It's been a long time since we last met. What are you doing here, and why are you dragging me out of my apartment?" Mary: "You were going to commit suicide! But why Violet?" Violet: "SUICIDE?! What? I was not going to do something like that. Why would I? It's so unreasonable". Just after a minute they saw from outside the apartment that her room was on fire. It was around 7:00 pm when that room caught fire.

CHAPTER 6
VIOLET IS SAVED

Violet: "Wow! My room is on fire! Does that mean you saved me Mary?" Mary: "We don't have time to discuss now. Let's go from here." Mary dragged Violet and she took her to her old apartment. Violet was very happy to meet Mary again and she told her many things that they did when she was away and how they were missing her a lot. Mary wasn't listening to her words because she also had to save Lucas from being murdered. She immediately asked: "Violet, do you know about Lucus and others?" Violet: "Oh! Lucas is living with Henry; they are roommates." Mary: "Can you please tell me the address? I want to go there." Violet told her the address and Mary headed out quickly to that address.

CHAPTER 7
THE MURDER

When she arrived there, she saw police cars outside and when she went to their room the police were gathered there. Lucas had already been murdered and Henry was handcuffed. The police were taking him to the car. She immediately went to the crime scene and saw Lucas' body lying there lifeless. She saw a bracelet there; she picked it up and kept it in her pocket. Suddenly everything started fading away from her memory and now she was at the place outside Violet's apartment again where she had saved her. After they went out again everything started disappearing from her memory.

CHAPTER 8
BACK TO THE FUTURE?

Mary woke up from her slumber. She immediately checked her phone, and it was 9th September 2023 again. She breathed a sigh of relief, got out of bed, freshened up and had her breakfast, but she was still thinking whether it was a dream or if she really had travelled to the past. After some time, the doorbell rang and her friends, including Kate, were at the door. She was extremely happy to see them and invited them in. They started talking and she noticed the bracelet on Kate's hand. She thought to herself, "I seemed to have seen this bracelet before!"

The End

PEOPLE VS. COVID-19
Ali Muhammad Waseem (Gr.11B)

The COVID-19 pandemic, which emerged in late 2019, has profoundly impacted the world in myriad ways. Initially causing widespread illness and loss of life, it strained healthcare systems globally. Lockdowns and travel restrictions disrupted economies, leading to job losses and business closures. Educational systems were upended, with millions of students forced into remote learning.Beyond the immediate health and economic effects, COVID-19 exposed societal vulnerabilities, including healthcare inequalities, inadequate preparedness for pandemics, and disparities in access to vaccines. It accelerated the adoption of remote work and digitalization while highlighting the importance of reliable internet connectivity.The pandemic also fueled misinformation and conspiracy theories, making it challenging to communicate accurate information. It underscored the importance of global cooperation in addressing public health crises, as vaccine distribution and variants crossed borders.As the world strives to recover, the enduring legacy of COVID-19 includes a reshaped work landscape, a renewed focus on public health, and a deeper understanding of our interconnectedness.

MY TRAVEL EXPERIENCE
Hammal Nasir (Gr. 6B1)

Hello everyone! My name is Hammal Nasir, and I am from Grade 6B1. Today I am going to   share my travel experience to Oman, so let's begin. It was winter holidays. We were at home and my dad gave us a surprise. He told us that we are going to a place in Oman with his friend's family and we will also be camping overnight there.

It was our first time, and we all were so very excited that we couldn't sleep. We woke up early in the morning and got ready for the journey.

Since it was winter the weather was lovely with slight rain. My father purchased all the camping equipment, like tents, air mattress, blankets, air pillows, rechargeable lights and all kitchen items required for the trip, as we were going to stay there for 2 days.

We started our journey in the morning, and we made some stops on the way. When we reached there, it was the 'WOW' moment! The place was surrounded with huge huts, crystal clear rivers and a beautiful dam along with play areas for kids and everything was free of charge.

We opened our tents and pitched them up in our area, propped up the chairs and took out all the camping accessories kitchen items.

There were specific areas assigned for barbecue. We barbecued, made, and had tea, played badminton, and we lit a bonfire in the night as it was cold.

In the morning we woke up and my mother and aunties made breakfast for us.

After having breakfast, we went hiking and had lovely photo shoots. It was such fun and we enjoyed the hiking along with my father's friend.

We went to the river which was near the dam, and we swam. Later in the evening, we played football. Next day, evening, we had our tea over there and then we tracked back home. I will never forget this wonderful trip.

BROKEN PROMISES
Lina Vazi Pinto [Gr. 11(AS)A]

When the heart shatters, and tears start to flow.

Anger begins to cloud all my judgment, as sadness and hurt grows.

My trust is shattered, as promises have faded.

While the betrayal's stings leave wounds, that leaves my feelings jaded.

Not sure if you meant anything that night, while I ask myself "why me?".

Wondering if this torture would ever end, and set my soul free.

No matter the tears, the heartbreak, the betrayal, you are still my 11:11 wish.

I want you for myself and no other, as you are the only man I ever want to kiss.

Letters in my hand gets read every night, as the words dagger my mind and drains my heart off tears. Knowing that all my nightmares came to life, in the form of my fears.

And as my heart heals, mending its broken parts. A new chapter unfolds, healing starts.

In time, the tears will dry off, and the pain will slowly fade. I will be happy again, as the love's light will shine a serenade.

I LOVE YOU SWEETHEART

Lina Vazi Pinto, 11 (AS) A

I see him from a distance,
Completely oblivious of my presence.
As I stare at his beautiful honey gaze, glistening with mischief
and excitement.

What did I do to not deserve such an angel in disguise? What
did I do to not get the most perfect man ever?
The man that no one else can compete with. Who makes me feel
safe and loved even when he's not around.

Whose voice mesmerizes me into a delusional reality where
it's just him and me. Us against the world.
Yet if I don't have him the way I need him. The way I ache for him.
I'd be content to set my wrist croaked upon the knife, Ready for
the countdown to come to an end, just so I can slice.

However, it is unfortunate how that beaming smile that he
is shining is blinding someone else's light. Someone he means
that smile for. She's right across him, happier than ever. I mean
how could she not be?

What did I do wrong for him to not be mine? Can he still be
mine?

I don't think I'll ever get the answer to that, but that doesn't
mean I'll lose hope. I'll always have hope.
Hope in us.

Anyways, it always was just lust right? Nothing more nothing
less, just lust right? A fantasy to think about late at night.

Even so, how can I hide my feelings from myself when I know
what I'm feeling will come to light, Only to torture and torment

me while it shoves a dagger through me and takes a bite.   As that's how much I love him.

I love him so much that I want nothing more than seeing him happy to the brim.

In fact, his ignorance makes My brain feel like two clouds pressed together, Expressing themselves by a change of weather. For numerous seconds, maybe even minutes, or hours, perhaps days, weeks, months, and many many crucial years.
Waiting with false hope that one day he will be mine.

I have convinced myself somehow that it could be possible,

But who knows who will get their hands on someone so divine.

I love you so much sweetheart more than words can express.

The only words I'd ever want to tell you at the altar by my side is, "yes". U make me feel loved, and safe.

You make my heart glow, brushing it with urs to chafe. U are a gem which is not to be lost.

Yet sadly I lost you but at what cost?

I love you so much sweetheart, and I'll never stop loving you.

Yours truly,

Your one in a few.

MARK MY WORD
Sarah Faisal, (Gr. 11A)

If you want to kill yourself, Jump in the ocean.

Mark my word,

You will find yourself trying to save yourself.

Then you will comprehend that you do not want
to kill yourself. It is the thought you want to kill.

Mark my word,

Death is not a solution.

Fighting it is important.

Kill what is killing you from the inside. And mark
my word,

Patience is important,

Remain patient you will get through it.

EDITORIAL

'Ponders & Pens'
Ms.Geredet Johnson

Amateur writers pen down their thoughts by way of articles, short stories, poems etc. It is with the start-up; the pick-up takes place. Fresh thoughts, jotted down in a jiffy, pondering on them later and converting them into readable content. To capture readers' interest is the aim of every writer.

We received several entries on a myriad of topics and choosing a handful was quite a difficult task. For the writers whose poems, stories, and articles we were not able to include, you are appreciated for your work, and you are urged to continue honing your writing skill.

The thoughts that go through one's mind, be it imaginative, creative, narrative, descriptive, objective, subjective and so on. It all adds up to the form of stories, poems, biographies, autobiographies, etc. all manifested in their writing. Letting imagination take wings!

From imagination to introspection, the thoughts of a writer encompass a range of characteristics that contribute to their ability to create extraordinary pieces of work. Within the realm of literature, there exists a fascinating connection between the minds of writers and the written pieces they create.

From the instance their pen touches the page, or their fingers play on the keyboard, their minds become a canvas where worlds are born, characters spring to life and emotions are skillfully woven into their artful writing, taking you to a world of infinite possibilities, delving into the realms of fantasies, reality, emotions, the future, time-travel, thriller, and it goes on.

Flipping through the pages of this book will take you through your school days of fun and frolic, reviving childhood memories, wishing one could time-travel to the days of the bygones. Wishful thinking!

Feelings have colors as is portrayed through the eyes of the child, the beautiful sunshine days, feeling the warmth of the sun on one's face. Colours galore, still to explore. Friends, favorites, wishes, travelling, promises, faith and how can we forget the COVID 19 that imprisoned everyone to stay put at home! Nevertheless, it was tamed! It's all in the game.

You will find beautiful pieces notable for their innovativeness, while there is no explicitly common theme. An interpretive eye, we hope will enjoy what is really a unique selection of tales in the form of poems, stories, and articles.

A subconscious 'child-like' attitude dwells within us, that which harnesses emotions, memories, and beliefs from the past as hopes and dreams of the future.

Let fantasy take wings, at the same time let reality keep us rooted.

www.ingramcontent.com/pod-product-compliance
Lightning Source LLC
Chambersburg PA
CBHW051503140726
47987CB00006B/2858